FUNDAMENTAL STUDIES

For

MALLETS

by

GARWOOD WHALEY

PREFACE

The purpose of this text is to provide the beginning student with studies which are both musically creative and technically progressive.

This volume is divided into three main sections.

SECTION I: PRELIMINARY STUDIES

Each of seventeen pages consists of technique, reading, and memorization. The simultaneous study of these elements will quickly develop the student's keyboard facility.

SECTION II: READING STUDIES

A collection of works by well-known composers, arranged for mallet instruments.

SECTION III: TECHNICAL STUDIES

A series of exercises which include major scales, major chords, minor scales, minor chords, and chromatic studies. These exercises may be used in conjunction with SECTION I or SECTION II.

This method will provide the beginning student with an interesting and progressive approach to the art of mallet playing.

To

KENDALL

BASIC PRINCIPLES

HAND POSITION

Hold the mallet firmly between the thumb and the first joint of the index finger. The third, fourth and fifth fingers should close around the mallet adding support to the grip. Both mallets are held alike.

PLAYING POSITION

Stand approximately six inches from the instrument and directly in the middle of the playing area.

STRIKING AREA

Strike the natural bars (A, B, C, D, etc.) directly in the center. The accidental bars (F#, G#, A#, etc.) should be struck near the end, never over the connecting cord.

THE ROLL

A roll is indicated by three slashes (♪). Rolls are produced by rapidly alternating single strokes (R L R L, etc.).

READiNG

It is extremely important not to look at the keyboard while reading. By concentrating on the music and not the keyboard, you will soon develop the necessary facility to become a proficient reader.

SECTION I

PRELIMINARY STUDIES

The purpose of this section is to provide the student with a multi-faceted, self-motivating approach to mallet playing. Through the integration of technical studies, reading, and memorization, the student's keyboard facility will quickly develop.

The memorization of recognizable or "rote" tunes is quite beneficial since it both motivates the student and develops his "keyboard motor skills." Students should be encouraged to memorize at least one piece per week. Each technical study should also be memorized.

TECHNIQUE

C major scale

L

READING

MEMORIZATION
(MARY HAD A LITTLE LAMB)

TECHNIQUE

C major triad

L

READING

MEMORIZATION
(TWINKLE, TWINKLE LITTLE STAR)

TECHNIQUE

READING

MEMORIZATION
(JINGLE BELLS)

8

Octaves

READING

MEMORIZATION
(LIGHTLY ROW)

TECHNIQUE

C chromatic scale

READING
(ENTRÉE)

LEOPOLD MOZART

Allegro

fine

D.C. al fine (Repeat to the beginning and play to the end [fine]).

MEMORIZATION
(LONDON BRIDGE)

TECHNIQUE

F major scale

L

READING
(ANGLAISE)

Allegro

LEOPOLD MOZART

fine

D.S. al fine

(see page 29)

MEMORIZATION
(FRÈRE JACQUES)

TECHNIQUE

F major triad

L

READING
(AYRE)

HENRY PURCELL

Andante

MEMORIZATION
(REUBEN, REUBEN)

TECHNIQUE

G major scale

READING
(RIGADOON)

Allegro

HENRY PURCELL

MEMORIZATION
(AIR)

Allegretto

MOZART

TECHNIQUE

G major triad

READING
(BOURRÉE)

Allegro

LEOPOLD MOZART

MEMORIZATION
(HUNGARIAN FOLK SONG)

TECHNIQUE

B♭ major scale

READING
(MINUET)

W.A. MOZART

Andante

MEMORIZATION
(AT PIERROT'S DOOR)

fine

D.C. al fine

TECHNIQUE

B♭ major triad

READING
(OLD FRENCH SONG)

PETER I. TSCHAIKOWSKY

MEMORIZATION
RAKES OF MALLOW

TECHNIQUE

D major scale

READING
(COUNTRY DANCE)

Allegro

BEETHOVEN

MEMORIZATION
(DECK THE HALLS)

TECHNIQUE

D major triad

R

READING
(HUNTER'S CHORUS)

Vivace

C.M. von WEBER

MEMORIZATION
(YANKEE DOODLE)

TECHNIQUE

Eb major scale

READING
(POLONAISE)

HEINRICH LICHNER

Allegro con gras

MEMORIZATION
(ODE TO JOY)

BEETHOVEN

Allegro Assai

TECHNIQUE

E♭ major triad

READING
(BAGATELLE)

BEETHOVEN

Allegretto

MEMORIZATION
(ANGELS WE HAVE HEARD ON HIGH)

TECHNIQUE

A major scale

READING
(GAVOTTE)

CORNELIUS GURLITT

Moderato

fine

D.S. al fine

dim.

MEMORIZATION
(MINUET)

Andantino

LEOPOLD MOZART

TECHNIQUE

A major triad
R

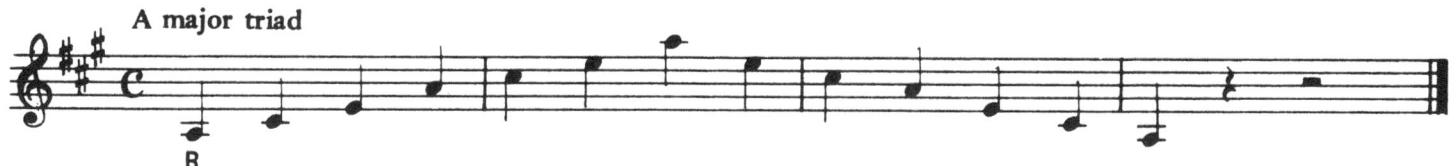

READING

(SONATINA)

KUHLAU

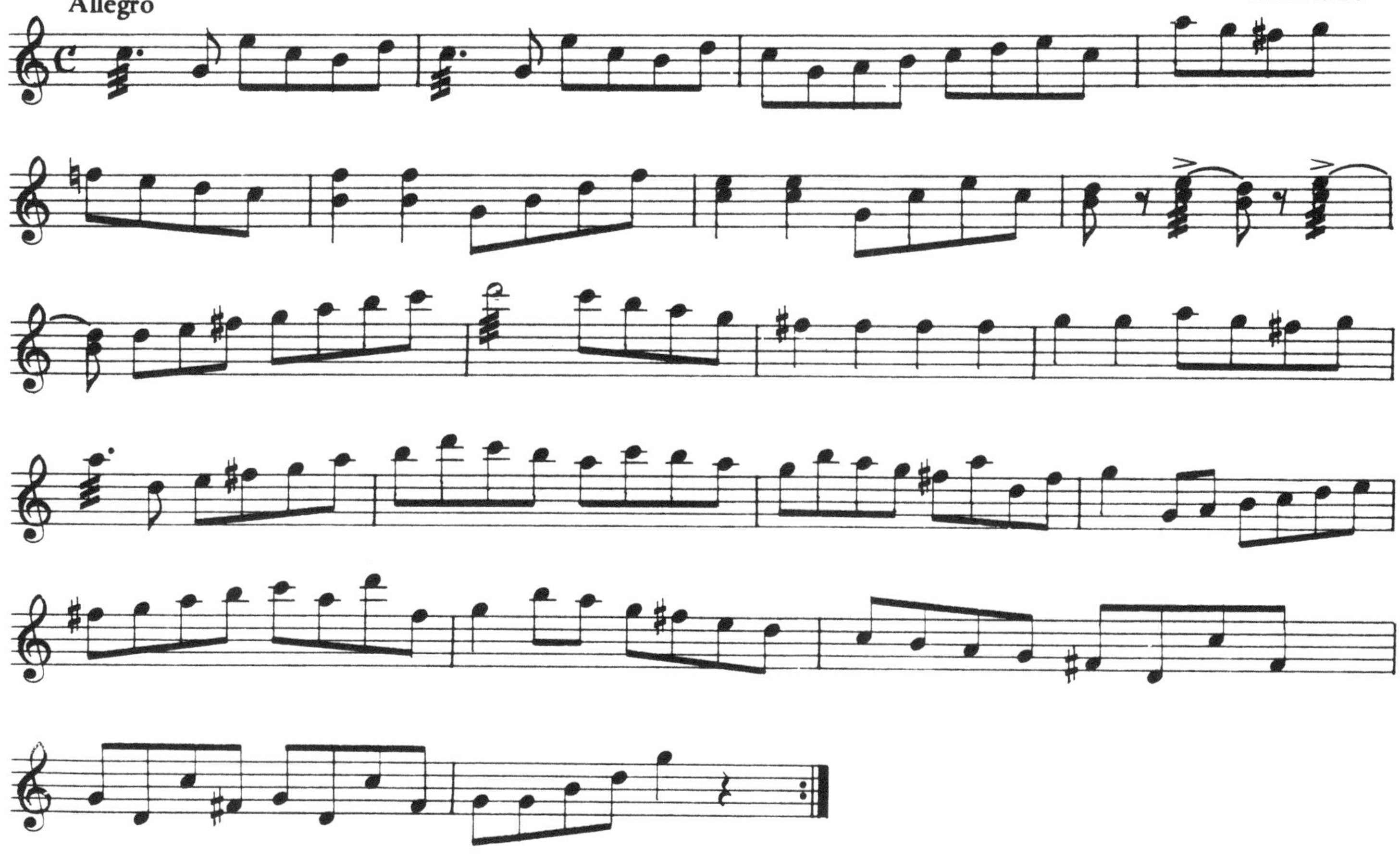
Allegro

MEMORIZATION

(MARCH from "AIDA")

VERDI

3
3
3
3
3

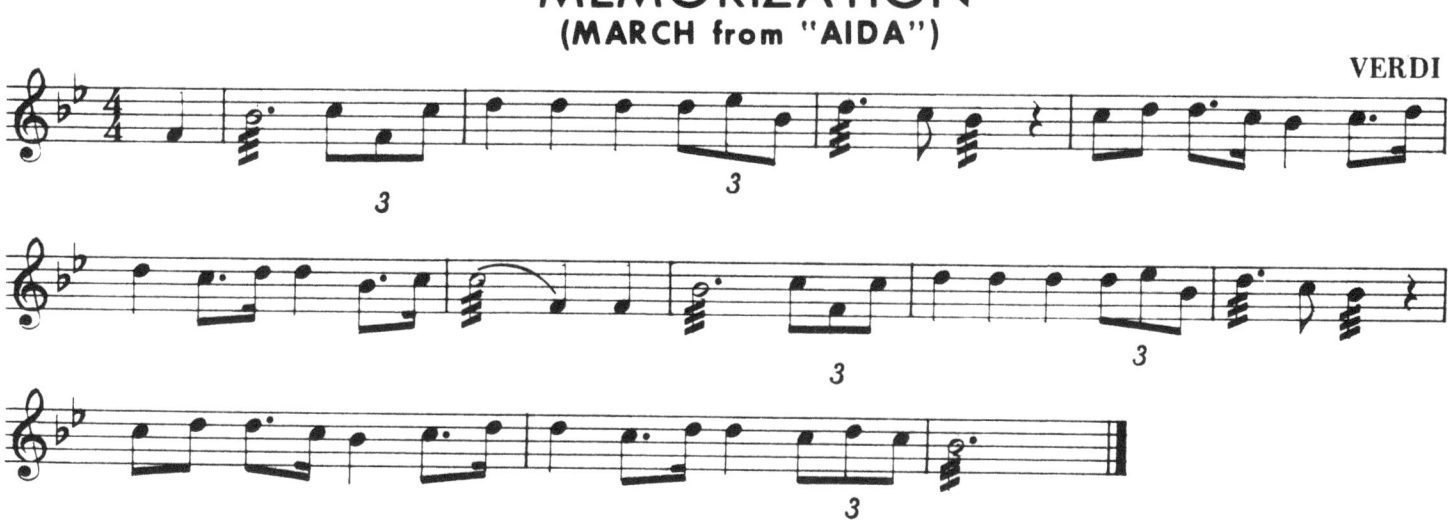

SECTION II

Reading Studies

The purpose of Section II is to provide the student with a progressive series of reading studies. The following music was selected on the basis of its adaptability to mallet instruments and for the aesthetic quality of each work. By perfecting each of the following pieces, the student will develop both reading skills and an appreciation for good music.

As a performance aid, stickings have been added during difficult passages. The teacher should however, feel free to alter these stickings to best suite the individual student.

Remember, the purpose of this section is to develop reading skills and basic musicianship. Each piece must be practiced slowly and carefully - concentrate on sound, not speed.

Notice that much of the musical material in this work is reused. Learn to recognize reoccuring passages as this will enable you to become a more proficient reader.

New Terms
Allegro: Quick
MF - Mezzo Forte: Moderately loud
Rit. - Ritardando: A gradual reduction of speed

IMPERTINENCE

GEORGE FREDERIC HANDEL

When playing "double stops" (two notes simultaneously) be sure that both notes are struck at exactly the same time.

New Terms
Vivace: Quick, lively
Risoluto: Resolute (bold)
F - Forte: Loud
FF - Fortissimo: Very loud
Cresc. - Crescendo - ⟨══════⟩ :   Gradually louder
Decresc. - Decrescendo - ⟨══════⟩ :   Gradually softer

MARCH

CORNELIUS GURLITT

A dot above or beneath a note head is a staccato mark and should be played in a short, detached manner using a snapping wrist motion. A dash above or beneath a note head is a tenuto mark indicating that the note should be held for its full rhythmic value.

New Terms
Allegretto: Quick
P - Piano: Soft
Poco Rit.: A little ritard

LE PETIT RIEN

FRANCOIS COUPERIN

The contrast in dynamics between measure four and measure five is extremely important. This dynamic contrast must be obvious to the listener.

SONATINA

MUZIO CLEMENTI

For rhythmic precision, dotted notes should always be sub-divided (count 1e&a). Carefully observe the dynamic changes throughout the following works.

New Terms

Andantino: Slightly faster than Andante

Dolce: Sweetly

Cantabile: Singing

SF - Sforzando: A sudden, strong accent

Dim. - Diminuendo: Gradually softer

Molto moderato: Very moderately

⌢ - Fermata: A pause

PASTORALE

FRIEDRICH BURGMÜLLER

MINUET

JOHANN SEBASTIAN BACH

ANDANTE

WOLFGANG AMADEUS MOZART

poco rit.

The natural articulation for most mallet instruments is staccato. By using a snapping wrist motion, it is possible to exaggerate this articulation. This is especially necessary during passages with loud dynamic levels.

New Terms
D.S. al Fine: Repeat to the sign (𝄋) and play to the end (Fine).
♪ - Staccato: In a detached manner; short

THE CLOCK

The Polonaise, a festive dance of Poland, should be played in a stately manner. Use a firm, controlled stroke.

The Bourrée, a 17th-century French dance, is usually quick and characterized by an upbeat. Use a snapping, staccato stroke.

POLONAISE

J.S. BACH

BOURRÉE

J.S. BACH

If the student's technique is sufficient, all quarter notes in this work should be rolled. Concentrate on making the "swells" (⟨———⟩ ⟨———⟩) as smooth and accurate as possible.

THE NEW DOLL

PETER TSCHAIKOWSKY

For a sensitive, musical performance of this work, carefully observe dynamic shading, tempo changes, and articulations.

SONATINA

HEINRICH LICHNER

Notice the stylistic differences between the following works. Approach each piece individually considering tempo, phrasing, articulations, and dynamics.

ANDANTE

MARCH

CAREFREE

DANIEL GOTTLOB TURK

This work contains many dynamic changes. Once a dynamic level has been established, it must remain constant throughout the work.

New Terms
Larghetto: Not as slow as Largo
Largo: Slow and broad

LARGHETTO

DOMENICO SCARLATTI

This work is rather difficult due to the many wide intervalic leaps. Because of this fact however, it is an excellent study for developing a "feel" for the keyboard. Remember, an accidental applies to the note in front of which it appears and lasts for one measure only.

PRELUDE #2

JOHANN SEBASTIAN BACH

Double stops, when played at a fast tempo, are usually difficult to play at exactly the same time. It is necessary for an accurate performance, however, to play these notes precisely together. Passages which are technically difficult, such as measures 21-28, must often be memorized.

LITTLE HUNTING SONG

Vivace

ROBERT SCHUMANN

38

Since much of the literature for mallet instruments is written in the upper register, the student should memorize leger lines as soon as possible.

New Terms
Scherzando: Playfully

ALLEGRETTO

FRANZ SCHUBERT

SECTION III

TECHNICAL STUDIES

The following section contains a series of technical exercises which include: major scales; major triads; natural, harmonic, and melodic minor scales; minor triads; and chromatic studies. These exercises should be memorized and incorporated into the student's daily practice routine.

Each of the following exercises should be praticed using both the indicated sticking and double-sticking. The ability to double-stick is extremely important and for technical facility, should be developed as soon as possible.

The technique of double-sticking is similar to the open double stroke snare drum roll. It is however, considerably more difficult since there is no natural rebound on mallet instruments.

Using a snapping wrist motion, practice each of the exercises as indicated below.

As a systematic approach to the exercises in this section, I suggest the following:

1. Memorize each exercise.
2. Practice slowly and evenly. Strive to produce a "musical" sound.
3. After mastering each exercise, begin using a metronome and increase the speed of each study by one or two beats per day.
4. Never let speed become the governing factor. The ultimate goal must always be to produce a well-balanced, "musical" sound.

MAJOR SCALES

MAJOR TRIADS

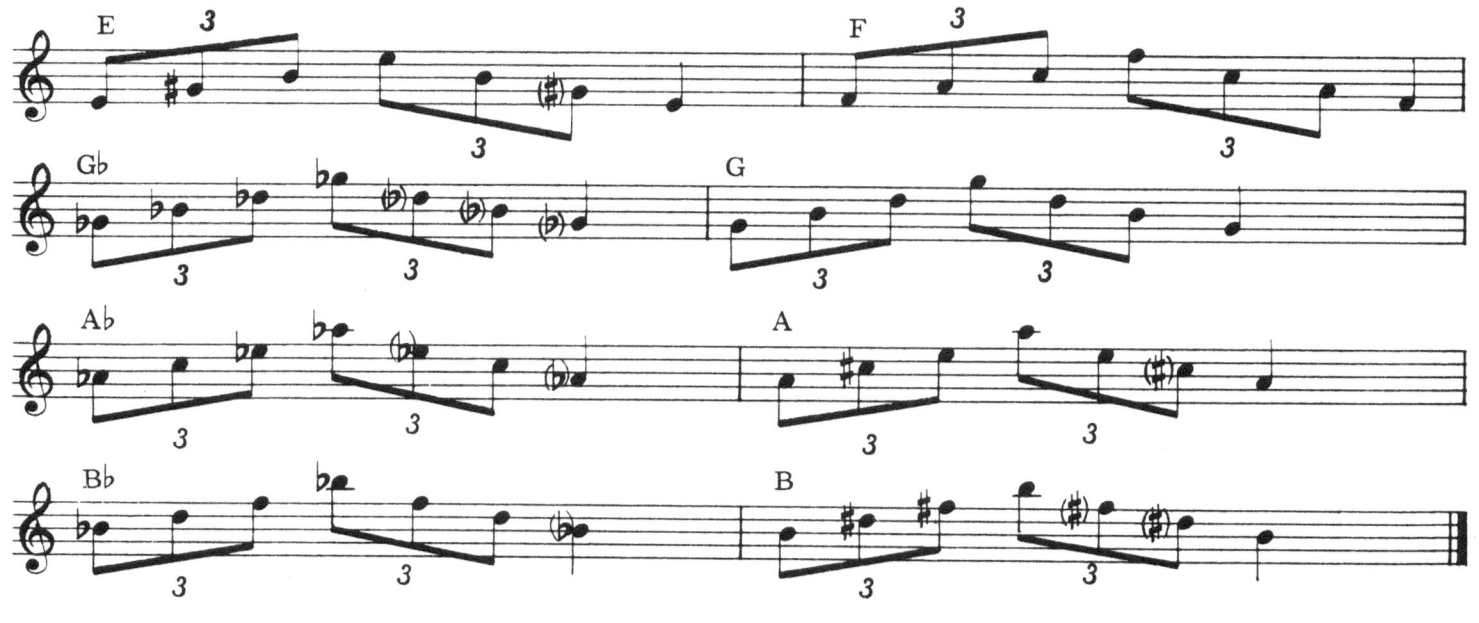

CHROMATC SCALE
(F - 2 OCTAVES)

CHROMATIC EXERCISE

THIRDS

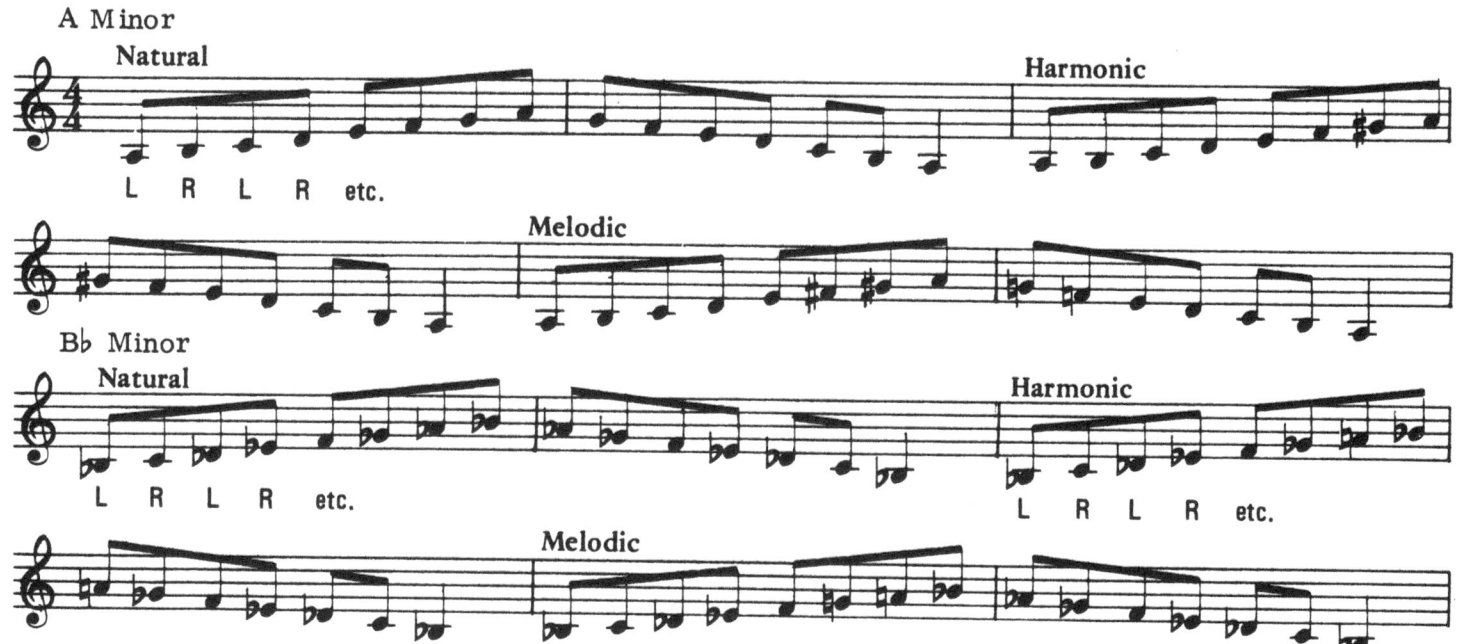

MINOR SCALES

44

MINOR TRIADS

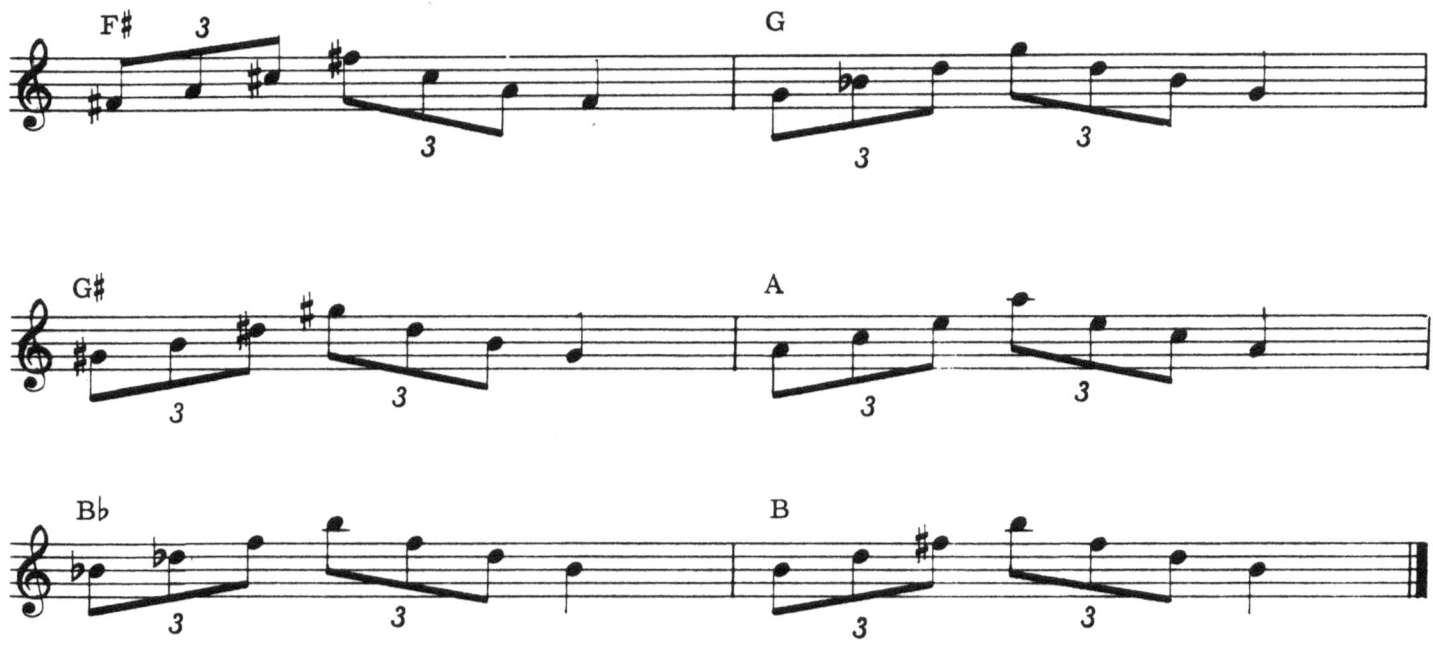

Other books by Garwood Whaley:

Fundamental Studies For Timpani
Fundamental Studies For Snare Drum
Musical Studies For The Intermediate Snare Drummer
Musical Studies For The Intermediate Timpanist
Intermediate Duets For Snare Drum
The Rhythmic Patterns Of Contemporary Music.

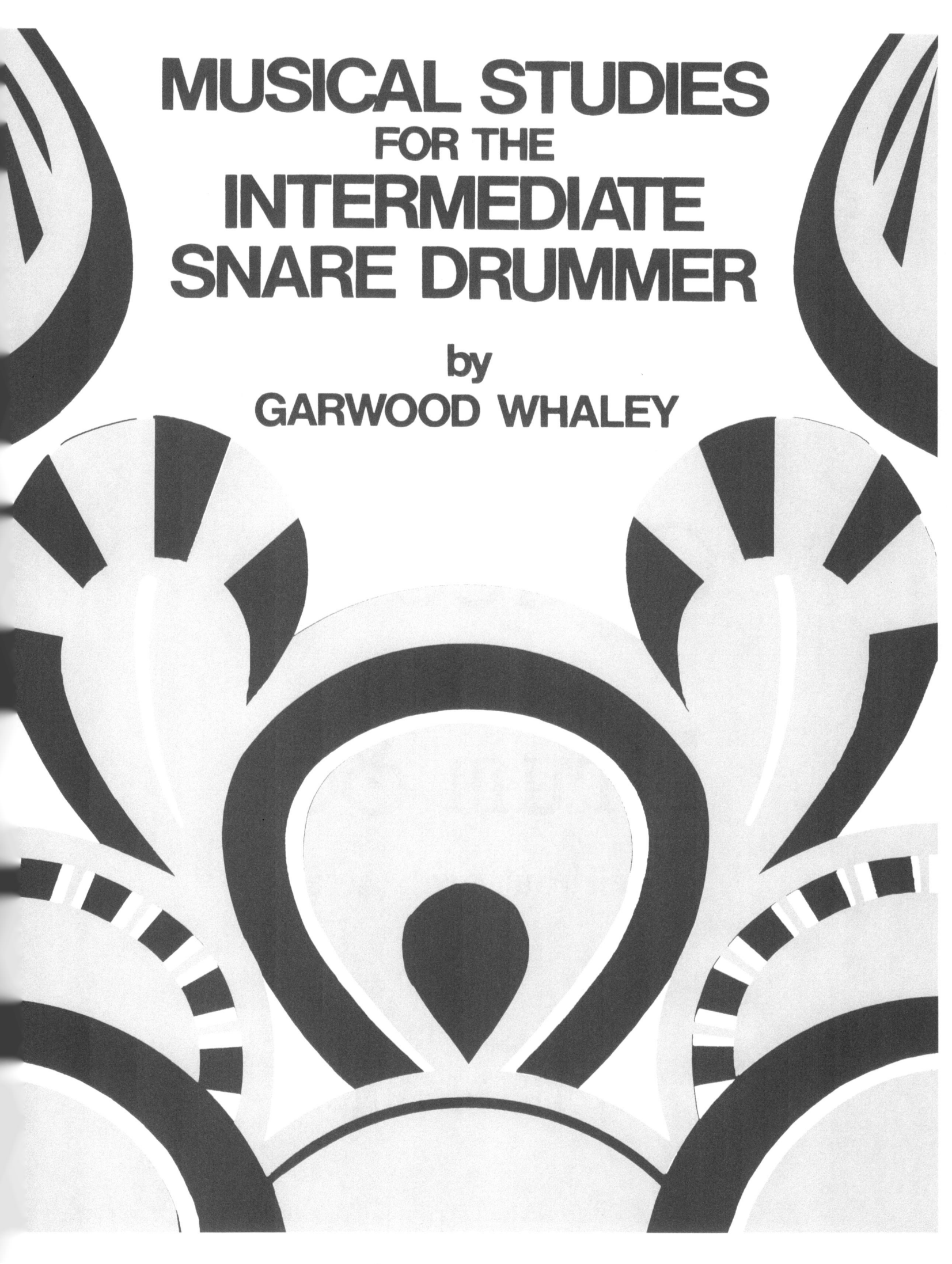

45 MINUTES, 33 SECONDS

Concerto
for
Drum Set

(without orchestra)

by
JOEL ROTHMAN